This Book Belongs To: Dugan Hubert

Date: 7-16-21

Published by: YM360

Next: Growing A Faith That Lasts
Copyright ©2015 by youthministry360. All rights reserved.

Published by youthministry360 in the United States of America.

ISBN 13: 978-1-935832-42-3
ISBN 10: 1935832425

No part of this publication may be reproduced, stored in a retrieval system, or transmitted in any form or by any means electronic or mechanical, including photocopy, recording, or any information storage and retrieval system now known or to be invented, without prior permission in writing from the publisher.

Any reference within this piece to Internet addresses of web sites not under the administration of youthministry360 is not to be taken as an endorsement of these web sites by youthministry360; neither does youthministry360 vouch for their content. Unless otherwise noted, all Scripture taken from the HOLY BIBLE, NEW INTERNATIONAL VERSION®. Copyright © 1973, 1978, 1984 Biblica. Used by permission of Zondervan. All rights reserved.

Author: Andy Blanks
Design: Upper Air Creative

CONTENTS

Next Intro — 1
Large Group Session 1 Notes — 3
Small Group Session 1 Intro — 5
Session 1 Getting Started — 6
Session 1 Digging In — 7
Session 1 Wrapping Up — 9
Large Group Session 2 Notes — 11
Small Group Session 2 Intro — 13
Session 2 Getting Started — 14
Session 2 Digging In — 15
Session 2 Wrapping Up — 17
Large Group Session 3 Notes — 19
Small Group Session 3 Intro — 21
Session 3 Getting Started — 22
Session 3 Digging In — 23
Session 3 Wrapping Up — 25
Large Group Session 4 Notes — 27
Small Group Session 4 Intro — 29
Session 4 Getting Started — 30
Session 4 Digging In — 31
Session 4 Wrapping Up — 33
Next Closing — 34
Devotion 1 — 35
Devotion 2 — 37
Devotion 3 — 39
Devotion 4 — 41

NEXT INTRO

At some point in your life you became a Christ-follower. You heard God's Truth and responded. You knew that you were a sinner and that your sin separated you from God. You learned that Jesus--perfect, holy Jesus--paid the once-and-for-all price for your sins, making peace between God and you. And in faith, you accepted His sacrifice on your behalf, submitting the leadership of your life to Christ, and entering into a relationship with God. At some point this happened to you. And it was amazing.

The problem is that for many of us, our stories don't go much further than this.

The problem is that this isn't how God intended our faith to look. God expects you to grow closer to Him. More than that, God expects you to be the one who cares the most about your spiritual growth. Over the next four sessions, you'll be shown how the Bible talks about a next level kind of faith. But this kind of faith isn't born overnight. It takes intentionality and a willingness to be moved and shaped by God.

Have You Prepared For The Journey?

Ask yourself: Is my heart prepared to hear God's voice? Am I willing to be changed? If you can't answer "yes" to these questions, this journey might not be nearly as spectacular as it could be. If you need to, take a moment and silently talk to God in prayer. Ask God to give you a heart that is open to His leading.

You're Holding Your Map

This book you're holding is the road map for your journey. It will help guide your experiences. Write your name and the date in the front. Hold on to it. You may want to look back and remember this time in your life.

Make An Impact, Be Impacted

Keep your eyes and ears open for those valuable moments where God seems to speak to you. But don't miss the chance to impact your friends, and to be impacted by them. Your friends are with you in this experience. Be open to what God is doing in and through them, and how He might be using them to speak to you. And vice versa.

Your journey to a next level faith is just beginning. Be prepared to be changed . . .

LET US RUN
with perseverance
the race marked out for us, **FIXING OUR EYES** on

Jesus

THE PIONEER & PERFECTER OF FAITH

Hebrews 12:1-2

Large Group Notes
Session 1

These two pages are designed for you to take notes on during Large Group Sessions. The stuff you're learning will really build on itself over the next few sessions. So even if you're not much of a note taker, you might want to at least jot down what you think is important.

Try writing down:
- Any specific teaching points
- Verse references for Scripture passages
- Quotes that make you think
- Anything you have a question about

Small Group Session 1 **Intro**

Think for a moment about the things you care most about.

For some of you this is athletics. For others it's your appearance. And for others, it may even be your grades.

Think about the way you approach the things you care about most. You probably don't have to be told to practice or to try hard in a game. You probably don't have to be reminded to do your hair or makeup. Most likely, no one is reminding you to study for the big test.

You take greater ownership in those areas of your life in which you care the most.

What if you were asked the same question about your faith? Who owns your spiritual growth? Who has the most ownership of the process by which you grow closer to Christ? Who is the person most responsible?

For many of you, if you were honest, the answer would be someone else. A parent or guardian. Or a youth worker. Maybe even a grandparent. For many of you, there is someone else in your life that pushes you, encourages you, and may very well (up to this point) care more about your relationship with Christ than you.

NEXT is out to help change that.

and it starts now.

Session 1 Getting Started
What's the next level? Answer the following questions as a group discussion.

Over the next few sessions, you'll be talking a lot about taking your faith to the next level. Let's spend a few minutes thinking about what the next level looks like in the real world.

For each of the scenarios listed below, discuss with your group what it would mean to go to the next level. (See how many "next levels" you can come up with for each.)

Scenario 1: The Athlete
You're a high school athlete in your chosen sport. What is the next level for you? What would it mean to continue to play after college?

A big deal

Scenario 2: The Actor
Let's say you like making movies with your friends. Or maybe your school has a drama club and you perform in plays. What is the next level for you? What would it mean to continue to excel as an actor?

A Big Deal

Scenario 3: The Designer
You love to design. Whether it's doodling, goofing around in Photoshop, painting, or creating pictures on your phone, if it's art, you love it. What is the next level for you? How do you continue to pursue your art as you grow up?

A Big Deal

Scenario 4: The Entrepreneur
You love to start things. Charities. Organizations. Food drives for the homeless. Businesses selling things you've made. What does the next level look like for you?

A Big Deal

Session 1 Digging In

Work with your group to read the passages and answers the questions below.

Part 1: Read Hebrews 5:11-14

[11] We have much to say about this, but it is hard to make it clear to you because you no longer try to understand. [12] In fact, though by this time you ought to be teachers, you need someone to teach you the elementary truths of God's word all over again. You need milk, not solid food! [13] Anyone who lives on milk, being still an infant, is not acquainted with the teaching about righteousness. [14] But solid food is for the mature, who by constant use have trained themselves to distinguish good from evil.

Can you pick up any clues in the text about the mood of the author? How would you describe the author's mood as he addresses his audience?

> *Frustrated.*

Why was he so frustrated? What was his biggest issue with his audience?

>

What would you think of a friend of yours who, instead of joining you at Taco Bell or wing night at your favorite restaurant, brought a baby bottle with him or her when you went out to eat?

> *I'd bring it up quickly.*

Why do you think some people are guilty of approaching their faith in the same way? In other words, why do you think so many teenagers come to faith in Christ but don't take their faith seriously enough to actually grow in their knowledge and love of God?

> *Go all the way*

Part 2: Read 1 Corinthians 3:1-3

¹Brothers and sisters, I could not address you as people who live by the Spirit but as people who are still worldly—mere infants in Christ. ²I gave you milk, not solid food, for you were not yet ready for it. Indeed, you are still not ready. ³You are still worldly. For since there is jealousy and quarreling among you, are you not worldly? Are you not acting like mere humans?

This is Paul writing to a different audience. And yet his argument is the same as the author of Hebrews. How are they similar?

Paul addresses the Corinthians' spiritual immaturity. He says they should be people who live by the Spirit. But instead they are living as worldly people. What do you think it means to live by the Spirit?

Why do you think he would describe the spiritually immature Corinthians as worldly?

Part 3: Read Hebrews 12:1-3

¹Therefore, since we are surrounded by such a great cloud of witnesses, let us throw off everything that hinders and the sin that so easily entangles. And let us run with perseverance the race marked out for us, ²fixing our eyes on Jesus, the pioneer and perfecter of faith. For the joy set before him he endured the cross, scorning its shame, and sat down at the right hand of the throne of God. ³Consider him who endured such opposition from sinners, so that you will not grow weary and lose heart.

What in your life "entangles" you, keeping you from growing in your faith as you should?

What insights does Paul share on how we can stay focused on growing our faith? (Hint: There are at least two.)

Session 1 Wrapping Up

This is your chance to start something new. Spend some time thinking about where your faith is and where you want it to be.

Where I Was in my Relationship with **Christ**

I was far from him

Where I Am in my Relationship with **Christ**

closer than I was

Where I Could Be in my Relationship with **Christ**

very close to him

HOW can they believe in the one of whom they HAVE NOT HEARD?

Romans 10:14

Large Group Notes
Session 2

These two pages are designed for you to take notes on during Large Group Sessions. The stuff you're learning will really build on itself over the next few sessions. So even if you're not much of a note taker, you might want to at least jot down what you think is important.

Try writing down:
- Any specific teaching points
- Verse references for Scripture passages
- Quotes that make you think
- Anything you have a question about

Small Group Session 2 Intro

Imagine one of your friends asks why you haven't responded to any of her texts. You look at your phone and inform her that you didn't get any of them. She asks if something is wrong with your phone. You tell her you don't think so, and ask if something is wrong with her phone. She answers, "Oh, I didn't send them on my phone. I sent them by writing them on paper airplanes and throwing them in your direction."

Why is this scenario so absurd? Because, pretty much all of our friends know that this isn't the way you send text messages. If you want to send a text message, you use a phone. In fact, we could say that one of the purposes of a phone is to send and receive messages.

Have you ever given the concept of "purpose" much thought as it applies to your life? Have you ever asked, "What is my purpose"?

Part of owning your faith is fully embracing the search for purpose.

If you're going to take your relationship with Christ to the next level, you can't do it without taking a step back and evaluating your purpose. Do you have a purpose? And if so, what is it? What are you here for? How will you use your life to make a difference?

The coolest thing? As someone who has committed his or her life to following Christ, you have an amazing purpose. Part of living a next level faith is understanding your purpose and embracing it. It's a crucial part of your faith-journey with Christ.

Session 2 Getting Started

Do what with what?! Work with your group to discuss the main ways you would use (and some ways you would definitely NOT use) the following objects.

Session 2 **Digging In**

Work with your group to process through this time of Bible study.

Take a moment and, in the space provided, define in your own words what you think the Gospel is.

Now, work with your group to discuss the following questions:
Listen as a few of your friends read their definitions. What common elements do you hear? What do you hear in other people's definitions that you left out?

Now let's compare your definition to a definition Paul gives us in his letter to the Romans.

Take a moment and read Romans 5:8-11.
⁸But God demonstrates his own love for us in this: While we were still sinners, Christ died for us. ⁹Since we have now been justified by his blood, how much more shall we be saved from God's wrath through him! ¹⁰For if, while we were God's enemies, we were reconciled to him through the death of his Son, how much more, having been reconciled, shall we be saved through his life! ¹¹Not only is this so, but we also boast in God through our Lord Jesus Christ, through whom we have now received reconciliation.

Answer these questions with your group:
Do you know what it means to be justified?

One more: Do you know what it means to be reconciled?

God justified you and reconciled with you even though you are a sinner. How does this make you feel?

You may be asking what this has to do with your purpose.

Great question. We're getting there. But first, take a moment to answer this question: Look at how Paul describes the impact of the Gospel on your life. Describe how the Gospel has changed your identity.

Now, read Romans 10:14-15.
14 How, then, can they call on the one they have not believed in? And how can they believe in the one of whom they have not heard? And how can they hear without someone preaching to them? 15 And how can anyone preach unless they are sent? As it is written: "How beautiful are the feet of those who bring good news!"

Answer these questions with your group:
Paul's words here actually have a great deal to do with your purpose. Can you get a feel from what Paul writes here what your purpose might be?

What does your purpose have to do with how you just described the Gospel's effect on your identity?

God may call you to be a preacher one day, and that would be really cool. But most of you won't be called to full time ministry. What are some examples of how you can "preach" the Gospel in your world each day?

What does it make you feel like knowing that God entrusts the sharing of the Gospel to you?

Remember This:
Taking your faith to the next level isn't possible without understanding, and embracing, your true purpose.

Session 2 Wrapping Up

How are you living out your purpose each day? Think of ways in which you communicate God's mission to the world around you.

Things I **Do**
- pray
- Read the bible

Things I **Say**
- Amen
- It's in his name

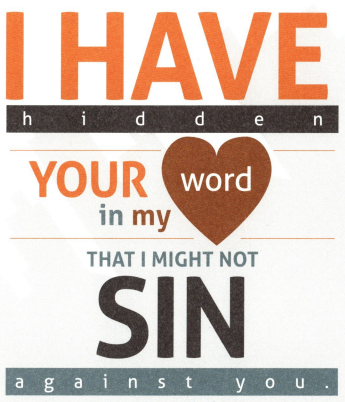

Large Group Notes
Session 3

These two pages are designed for you to take notes on during Large Group Sessions. The stuff you're learning will really build on itself over the next few sessions. So even if you're not much of a note taker, you might want to at least jot down what you think is important.

Try writing down:
- Any specific teaching points
- Verse references for Scripture passages
- Quotes that make you think
- Anything you have a question about

Small Group Session 3 **Intro**

What do you do that requires practice? School? Sports? Video games? Something creative?

While a lot of people don't particularly enjoy practice (especially as much as they enjoy the games), practice is essential if we want to improve. Practice is the act of developing and/or refining specific skills through focus and repetition. Practice helps you develop the skills you need to be successful at whatever it is you're pursuing.

So, what does this have to do with taking your faith to the next level?

So far in this study, you've been challenged to take greater ownership of your faith; and you've learned that a big part of this is living out your purpose as a part of God's mission. You're going to spend this session focusing on the backbone of next level faith ownership, what we'll call next level habits. Just like practice helps you develop the skills necessary to be proficient in sports or school, these next level habits will help you develop the foundation you need to own your faith and pursue your purpose.

Session 3 Getting Started

Listed below are five positive outcomes. For some or all of them, work with your group to identify three to five critical things that would have been crucial to successfully pulling them off.

1. You got elected class president.

2. She said "yes" when you asked her to go to prom.

3. You beat/completed the video game.

4. Your parents bought you the new car you asked for.

5. You made the cheerleading squad.

Session 3 Digging In

What does it take to build a next level faith? Get ready to dig in and find out.

If you had to guess what the four or five most import spiritual habits were, what would your answer be?

Spiritual Habit 1: _____

Read Psalm 119:9-16:
⁹ How can a young person stay on the path of purity? By living according to your word. ¹⁰ I seek you with all my heart; do not let me stray from your commands. ¹¹ I have hidden your word in my heart that I might not sin against you. ¹² Praise be to you, LORD; teach me your decrees. ¹³ With my lips I recount all the laws that come from your mouth. ¹⁴ I rejoice in following your statutes as one rejoices in great riches. ¹⁵ I meditate on your precepts and consider your ways. ¹⁶ I delight in your decrees; I will not neglect your word.

- What clues do you see here about the author's attitude toward interacting with God's Word?
- Can you think of a time in your life where you felt any of these same emotions about God's Word?

Spiritual Habit 2: _____

Read Psalm 5:3 and Psalm 88:13.
In the morning, Lord, you hear my voice; in the morning I lay my requests before you and wait expectantly.
– Psalm 5:3

But I cry to you for help, Lord; in the morning my prayer comes before you.
–Psalm 88:13

- What can we tell about the author's attitude toward prayer?
- Are you brave enough to describe your own attitude toward prayer? Is it similar or different from the author's attitude in these psalms?

Spiritual Habit 3: _____

Read Hebrews 12:28 and Psalm 29:2.
Therefore, since we are receiving a kingdom that cannot be shaken, let us be thankful, and so worship God acceptably with reverence and awe.
– Hebrews 12:28

Ascribe to the Lord the glory due his name; worship the Lord in the splendor of his holiness.
– Psalm 29:2

- What can we tell about the author's attitude toward worship?
- Describe how worship draws you closer to God.

Spiritual Habit 4: _____

Read Ephesians 6:7 and Colossians 3:23-24.

Serve wholeheartedly, as if you were serving the Lord, not people.
– Ephesians 6:7

Whatever you do, work at it with all your heart, as working for the Lord, not for human masters, since you know that you will receive an inheritance from the Lord as a reward.
– Colossians 3:23-24

- What is our attitude toward service supposed to reflect?
- How can our attitudes toward service become misplaced?

Growing a next level faith **doesn't happen** without a firm foundation of **solid spiritual habits.**

Session 3 **Wrapping Up**

In what area(s) do you need to focus on drawing closer to Christ? Spend some time thinking of how you might get more serious about your spiritual habits.

Bible Reading

Prayer

Worship

Service

Don't let anyone look DOWN on you because **you are young** but set an example for the **BELIEVERS** in *conduct*, in *love*, in *faith* and in *purity*.

1 Timothy 4:12

Large Group Notes
Session 4

You know what to do with these two pages by now, right? Use them to take notes during your Large Group sessions. By now you've figured it out: this stuff matters! This could be a time in your life you look back on as pretty important. So, write down anything that stands out to you as something you might want to hold on to.

Try writing down:
- Any specific teaching points
- Verse references for Scripture passages
- Quotes that make you think
- Anything you have a question about

Small Group Session 4 Intro

Here you are, almost finished.

You've arrived at your last session of NEXT. You've been building to this point. You're ready to push through to the finish, learning where all this talk of a next level faith is leading you.

In this final session, you're going to be sent out with an important challenge. This final session focuses on one key concept: influence.

We've been building to this point, even if you didn't know it. In Session 1, you learned how vital it is for you to take an increased ownership in your faith. In Session 2, you learned how living out your purpose is a huge part of having a greater level of faith-ownership. Session 3 taught you how important good spiritual habits are in laying the foundation for a life of purpose. And in this final session, you're going to see the culmination of all these things.

When you take greater ownership of your faith, and when you're living out your purpose fueled by solid spiritual practices, your life takes on a new and deeper level of potential impact. Your influence will grow.

Influence. It's the concept we'll be focusing on this session. You have more influence than you know. Your life has more potential than you give yourself credit for.

Session 4 Getting Started

Who has the most influence? Work with your group to answer the following questions.

Who are the **most influential people** you can think of in the following categories?

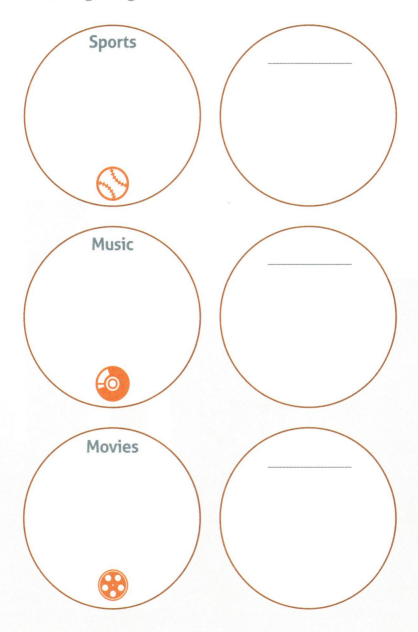

Session 4 **Digging In**

What does influence have to do with a next level faith? Work with your group to see what the Bible has to say.

Read 1 Timothy 4:12.

[11] Command and teach these things. [12] Don't let anyone look down on you because you are young, but set an example for the believers in speech, in conduct, in love, in faith and in purity.

What is it about being young that makes people quick to dismiss the impact you can potentially have on the world?

Paul provides a suggestion for how to keep people from minimizing your influence because of your age. What solution does Paul offer?

In your own words, what does it mean to set an example for others?

In the original Greek, the phrase set an example means, "to serve as a pattern." What does this have to do with our discussion on influence?

Speech

Conduct

Love

Faith

Purity

Session 4 Wrapping Up

Who do you influence? Take a moment to think about who you influence and the kind of impact you are making on their lives.

Not everyone is a leader. But EVERYONE HAS INFLUENCE.

NEXT Closing

You've come to the end of this study. Hopefully by now you have a good idea of what it means to live a next level faith. But there's one more thing you need to be reminded of: As you think about taking your faith to the next level, it may be tempted to put it off. Don't. Don't wait until you're older to start impacting the world around you for the sake of Christ.

Your life today, right now, is so full of potential. The idea that you need to wait until you know more, or are more mature, or are more put together, or are more popular is simply a lie. Your influence may increase as you get older. But that doesn't mean that God wouldn't love to unleash your potential on the world today. Because He would. He really would.

But this type of influence doesn't happen unless you're committed to growing in your faith.

Make owning your faith a primary goal in your life.

Pursue a closeness with God.

Seek Him daily.

Let your life be a bright light in the world around you.

Make a difference.

And start. Right. **Now.**

NEXT Devotion One

This is the first of four NEXT devotions. Find some time to work through them during your study of NEXT.

Read Joshua 4:1-7. The Israelites have just finished their four-decades-long tour of the desert, and have finally entered the land God had promised them. It was a big deal. And so Joshua told them to do something special. He told them to make a marker, a pile of stones, to commemorate this epic event in the course of their faith-journey with God. Joshua told them that in the future, they'd be able to see these stones and remember a time when God was super-faithful to them.

Here's a true statement: If you stay close to God throughout your life, you will have spiritual markers (just like the Israelites and their stack of rocks) where you can look back and see evidence of God doing something awesome in your life.

What if this time were one of those times for you? What if you could look back at this time and say this was when you got serious about your faith?

Are you ready to take that next step?

Are you ready to take ownership of your faith journey?

Are you willing to put Christ first in your life?

If you're serious about seeing your faith truly become a real presence in your life, look over at the next page.

Something To Think About . . .

If you're ready for this to be an important spiritual marker in your life, take a moment and write a prayer to God, expressing your desires to take your faith to the next level.

Now, trust that God will honor your desires. Trust that the Holy Spirit will work within you to draw you closer to God, making you more like Him in the process.

Now, here's your challenge: Come up with a marker to remember this moment, kind of like the Israelites did with the rocks. You can use the space below to draw a picture. You can go find a rock and put it on your desk or bathroom counter. Take a picture of something interesting or beautiful and make it your phone's screensaver. Write a poem. Make a sculpture. Whatever you do, take the time to mark this moment. It may very well turn out to be a turning point in your faith.

**End this activity by spending some time in silent reflection.
Listen to God. Praise Him.
Reflect on this change you're making in your life.**

NEXT Devotion Two

This is the second of four NEXT devotions. Find some time to work through them during your study of NEXT.

Take a moment and read Matthew 21:18-22. Jesus had just spent the previous day in Jerusalem where He would celebrate His final Passover with His disciples before He would be arrested and crucified. Jesus left Jerusalem to spend the night in the city of Bethany. The exchange with the fig tree happened as the disciples and Jesus were headed back into Jerusalem the next morning. Jesus was primarily teaching the disciples about the power of faith. But there's something here to be learned about our purpose as well.

What does this story have to do with your purpose?

Ask yourself, why was Jesus frustrated? He was frustrated because He expected the fig tree to have figs. Why? Because producing figs was the tree's purpose. That's pretty much all it was designed to do. Jesus rightfully expected the tree to live out its purpose. And when it didn't, He was frustrated.

Now, Jesus won't make you wither up if you don't live out your purpose. He won't. But Jesus expects you to live a life of purpose. Like the fig tree, you were designed with a purpose. When you fail to be who you were designed to be, you fail to honor God and the role He wants you to play in His rescue mission. You were created for a reason. Jesus died a purposeful death so you could live a purposeful life. Just going through the motions won't cut it.

Something To Think About . . .

Take a moment and read through the following questions. Write your answers in the space provided if you want. If you don't feel like writing, at least take a few moments to consider your answers.

In your own words, what does pursuing the purpose God has for you and your life have to do with taking your faith to the NEXT level?

Can you think of some examples of what it looks like for a teenager NOT to pursue his or her purpose?

Jesus won't wither you up like He did the fig tree. (At least I hope He won't.) But there seems to be consequences for us when we fail to grow in our faith and live our lives as a part of God's rescue mission. What might some of these consequences be?

End this activity by spending some time worshipping God in prayer. Thank Him for expecting you to play a part of His mission, and for giving you the opportunity to do so.

Ask Him to give you the strength you need to seek out your purpose by getting on board with His mission.

NEXT Devotion Three

This is the third of four NEXT devotions. Find some time to work through them during your study of NEXT.

Read Psalm 119:9-16. Can you feel the passion the author has for God and His Word?

Ask yourself this question: Do I realistically think it's possible for me to have this same passion for God and His Word?

It IS possible for you to have this level of passion about reading the Bible, you know. But first, you have to begin by breaking down a preconceived notion many people have about the Bible. What is it? It's this:

> **Reading your Bible isn't a chore. It's not a box to be checked off. Opening your Bible and reading it is an appointment with God Himself. If the Bible is God's main way of making Himself known to us, then reading the Bible is the closest we'll get this side of Heaven to knowing Him. You absolutely, 100% have to stop seeing your quiet time as a task, and see it as a chance to meet God in the pages of the Bible.**

Here's the deal: Most of us view our daily quiet time as a chore, a task we have to do because we know we're supposed to do it. We have to do it and if we don't do it we feel guilty and terrible and like we're not a good Christian like everybody else. This kind of thinking is exhausting. And it's the exact opposite of how God wants us to feel.

If this describes you, you need to re-think how you connect with God in His Word. Your challenge right now is to spend some time meditating on the verses on the following page (that simply means read them and think about them), asking God to create in you the same passion for knowing Him and His Word as is reflected in these verses.

Something To Think About . . .

> You will seek me and find me when you seek me with all your heart.
> – Jeremiah 29:13

> Open my eyes that I may see wonderful things in your law.
> – Psalm 119:18

> Direct me in the path of your commands, for there I find delight.
> – Psalm 119:35

> But his delight is in the law of the LORD, and on his law he meditates day and night. He is like a tree planted by streams of water, which yields its fruit in season and whose leaf does not wither. Whatever he does prospers.
> – Psalm 1:2-3

> Glory in his holy name; let the hearts of those who seek the LORD rejoice. Look to the LORD and his strength; seek his face always.
> – 1 Chronicles 16:10-11

NEXT Devotion Four

This is the fourth and final NEXT devotion. Find some time to work through them during your study of NEXT.

Evangelism, or sharing the Gospel with those who don't know Christ, is one of the core habits in owning a NEXT level faith. It's interesting how culture has impacted how people share and receive discussions about faith. Generations ago, it was more culturally acceptable to simply walk up to a stranger and ask something like, "If you died tonight, where would you spend eternity?" More often than not, you'd have an engaging conversation. And while there was certainly no guarantee of someone coming to faith in Christ, the conversation stood a fairly good chance of being effective, if not at least well-received.

Times have changed.

Many people who study this sort of thing have been saying for a while that these types of conversations aren't nearly as effective in our current culture. While this may be true, it's important that we never put limitations on the Holy Spirit. God may very well lead you to approach strangers and talk about your faith. And God may have been working on these people's hearts ahead of time. And you may find yourself leading someone you just met to Christ in the middle of Target's parking lot. This happens. But when you consider how our culture has changed, you may find that what people refer to as "relational evangelism" may be more effective. Which brings us to the idea of influence and evangelism.

Read Acts chapters 24-26. Yeah, I know. Two chapters. But it's a quick read and a very cool story. Take three minutes to read the chapters and look at page 42 for some follow up questions.

Something To Think About . . .

OK, so I am trusting that you read those chapters. In them, you saw Paul on trial defending himself against the accusations of the Jews. Paul appeared before three different Roman officials over the course of what many believe may have been a few years. Over this time, Paul developed a sort of relationship with these rulers. Now, the weren't all BFF. But, Paul used what relationship he had to influence them and to share the Gospel.

Go back and find the places where Paul shared the Gospel with the various leaders. (You don't have to write it down if you don't want. Just refresh your memory.)

1. How do you see Paul using his influence for God's glory?

2. Would you say Paul was in an ideal situation? Why do we sometimes hesitate to share the Gospel? What keeps us from using our influence to spread God's name?

3. Have you had opportunities lately to share the Gospel that you passed up? What would you do differently next time?

4. What are three things you can learn from how Paul handled himself in these chapters?

5. What are three things you can learn from how Paul handled himself in these chapters?

WHAT KEEPS YOU FROM BEING ALL THAT GOD HAS CALLED YOU TO BE?

Whatever it is, you need to know this: there is a better way. God wants you to face your fears and lean-in to who He desires you to be. If you're ready, Facing Your Fears is a great place to start.

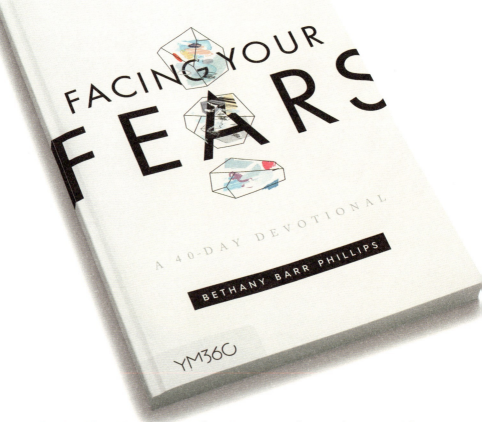

Facing Your Fears, a 40-day, Scripture-driven devotional by Bethany Barr Phillips, helps reveal where fear has taken hold of your life and equips you to put an end to these strongholds.

TO VIEW SAMPLES OF *FACING YOUR FEARS* & TO ORDER, GO TO YM360.COM/FEARS

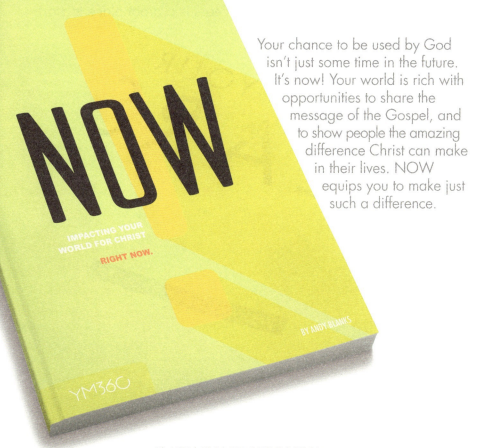

YOU HAVE AMAZING POTENTIAL TO IMPACT YOUR WORLD FOR CHRIST.

NOT TOMORROW. RIGHT NOW!

Your chance to be used by God isn't just some time in the future. It's now! Your world is rich with opportunities to share the message of the Gospel, and to show people the amazing difference Christ can make in their lives. NOW equips you to make just such a difference.

"NOW" WILL HELP YOU...
- Understand the PURPOSE God has in store for you
- Catch God's VISION for exactly how He wants to use you
- PRACTICE real, practical ways to impact your world
- Commit to ACTING on the opportunities God is giving you

TO VIEW SAMPLES OF NOW & TO ORDER, GO TO YM360.COM/NOW

About the **AUTHOR**

Andy is the Co-Founder and Publisher for YM360. Andy lives in Birmingham, AL with his wonderful wife Brendt, their three daughters, and one son. He's a pretty big fan of both the Boston Red Sox and anything involving the Auburn Tigers. When he's not hanging out with his family or volunteering at his church's youth ministry, you can find Andy trail running or mountain biking.